EARTH IN DANGER!

Energy

Polly Goodman

HODDER
Wayland

an imprint of Hodder Children's Books

Titles in the **EARTH IN DANGER!** series

Coasts   Rivers

Energy   Settlements

Farming   Transport

For more information on this series and other Hodder Wayland titles, go to www.hodderwayland.co.uk

This book is a simplified version of the title *Energy* in Hodder Wayland's 'Earth Alert' series.

Language level consultant: Norah Granger
Editor: Belinda Hollyer
Designer: Jane Hawkins

First published in 2001 by Hodder Wayland,
an imprint of Hodder Children's Books.

This paperback edition published in 2005

Britian Library Cataloguing in Publication Data
Goodman, Polly
Energy. - (Earth in danger!)
1. Power resources - Juvenile literature
I. Title
333.7'9
ISBN 0 7502 4729 0

Printed in China by WKT Company Limited

Hodder Children's Books
A division of Hodder Headline Limited
338 Euston Road, London NW1 3BH

Picture acknowledgements
Cover: main picture Robert Harding, solar panels Hodder Wayland Picture Library; Axiom Photographic Agency (Jim Holmes) 20, (Jim Holmes) 28; James Davis Travel Photography 3; Ecoscene (Angela Hampton) 18, (Nick Hawkes) 25; Eye Ubiquitous 4 bottom; Hodder Wayland Picture Library 6, 8 top, 12, 17 bottom, 27; Impact Photos (Mark Henley) 1, (Tony Page) 5, (Jorn Stjerneklar) 8 bottom, (Homer Sykes) 9, (Yann Arthus Betrand) 10, (Peter Arkell) 11, (Charles Coates) 16, (Mark Henley) 19, (Javed A Jaferji) 22; W. Lord 26; Sheffield City Council 23 both; Splash Communications 21 both; (David Young Wolff) 4 top, (Mike Abrahams) 7, (Ken Graham) 13, (Tony Craddock) 17 top, (Dave Jacobs) 24; Trip (M Watson) 14.
Artwork by Peter Bull Art Studio.

Contents

What is energy?

We need energy to do things. We use energy all the time and in many different forms.

When you were asleep last night, your body used energy to keep your heart pumping. When you got out of bed, the muscles in your legs used energy to let you walk. If you had breakfast, your toaster used energy to make bread into toast, and the fridge used energy to keep the milk cool. If you travelled to school by bus or car, your transport used energy.

We use energy to make our bodies move and work. We also use energy for heating, lighting, cooking, transport, and to run machines.

▲ Some things we use at home, such as irons, use energy from electricity.

Computers use energy from electricity. ▶

Damage from energy

We use a huge amount of energy. The way we make and use some forms of energy can damage the environment. Many scientists believe we are in danger of running out of energy sources.

We need to find out which types of energy are the least harmful. We also need to find ways of cutting down the amount of energy we use.

▲ Smoke from an oil refinery pollutes the air with gases.

Activity

ENERGY DIARY

Keep an energy diary for a week. Each day, write a list of everything you do and where the energy it used came from. Use the example below as a guide.

TIME	ACTIVITY	TYPE OF ENERGY
0730	Ate toast for breakfast	Electricity and my body
0800	Bus to school	Diesel

Sources of energy

- The wind, the sun and moving water are renewable sources of energy.
- Coal, oil and gas are non-renewable sources of energy.

Two farmers use energy from their bodies and from a machine to plant rice. ▼

Most of the earth's energy comes from the sun. Energy in the sun's rays helps plants to grow, and plants provide food for people and animals. Food is used to make our muscles work, which helps us survive.

The sun's energy is stored in wood, coal, oil and gas. These are called fuels. We burn fuels to release their energy, which we use to drive machines and to make electricity.

Other sources of energy are the wind, the sun and moving water.

Fuels

Wood is the oldest type of fuel. For centuries it has been burned for cooking and heating. It is still used in poorer countries, where people cannot afford more expensive fuels.

Coal, oil and gas are called fossil fuels. They were formed over millions of years from the fossilized remains of plants and animals.

Coal is made from the remains of plants, squashed together in layers. Oil and gas are formed from plants and animals that died in the sea. Fossil fuels have been used to power machines since the 1700s.

▲ A coal miner deep underground.

▲ An oil drill about to enter the ground.

Problems with fossil fuels

Fossil fuels are non-renewable sources of energy because it would take millions of years to replace them. They also cause air pollution when they are burned.

Water

Water is used to make electricity, or hydropower. Dams built across rivers collect water in reservoirs. The water falls through turbines in the dam, which turn the energy into electricity.

Dams raise the water level in rivers, so the water falls further and makes more energy. ▼

OIL UNDER THE CASPIAN SEA

Oil is so valuable that it can cause wars between countries.

The Caspian Sea is a large sea in Central Asia. It is surrounded on all sides by Russia, Kazakhstan, Turkmenistan, Iran and Azerbaijan.

There are vast amounts of oil under the Caspian Sea, and the countries around it are arguing over who owns it. Some of these countries have been at war with each other for years. Arguments over oil could make these wars worse, or cause new wars to break out.

If the countries agree about who owns the oil, new pipelines will have to be built to carry the oil to Europe and Asia.

An oil rig at sea is often as big as a small town. ▶

Nuclear energy

Nuclear energy is made from uranium, which is a type of rock. The energy is made by splitting the nucleus of the uranium atom. Then power stations turn the energy into electricity.

Nuclear energy can be very dangerous if it is not carefully controlled. It gives off radioactivity, which damages all living things.

Inside a nuclear power station. ▶

ENERGY THEN & NOW

In Britain today we have more sources of energy than in 1850. Then, people burned wood and coal. Now we use oil, gas, nuclear and water power.

Electricity

Electricity is made from different energy sources, by generators in power stations. Coal, gas, oil and nuclear power stations use heat to make steam, which turns the generators. Water turns the generators in hydroelectric power stations.

Energy around the world

Fossil fuels such as oil, gas and coal are not found all around the world. Countries where they are found, like Britain and the USA, have grown rich by using the fuels for transport and industry. They have also made money by selling the fuels to other countries.

In some countries, many people cannot afford to buy fossil fuels. They still rely on animals to pull machines, and use wood for cooking and heating.

Some of these countries are finding other ways to make their own energy, such as hydropower. They are borrowing money to build hydropower stations.

Fossil fuels help industry, like this car factory. ▼

Activity

ENERGY MAP

1. Trace a map of Britain.
2. Draw symbols showing the location of coal mines and power stations, using information from your local library.
3. Show whether the power stations use coal, water, gas or nuclear energy to produce electricity.

Problems of energy

Making and using energy can damage the environment in different ways. Some forms of energy are more harmful than others.

Running out of energy

Fossil fuels such as coal, oil and gas are non-renewable. Many people believe that if we carry on using these fuels as much as we do today, they will start to run out in fifty years' time. The chart on the left shows how much time we have left.

ENERGY CLOCK

This chart shows the estimated number of years left before the earth runs out of energy sources.

Oil	45 years
Natural gas	65 years
Black coal	190 years
Brown coal	300 years

An open coal mine in Germany. ▼

Transporting fuels

Fuels are carried huge distances, by lorries, tankers and pipelines. This transport can damage the environment.

Engines in lorries and tankers burn even more fossil fuels and gases pollute the atmosphere. Oil leaks from tankers and pipelines kill wildlife and pollute the water. It can take many years for a region to recover from an oil spill.

An oil pipeline crossing Alaska. ▼

Producing electricity

When coal, oil or gas power stations produce electricity, they release gases into the air, causing air pollution. Nuclear power stations also produce waste, which stays very dangerous for thousands of years. People are still looking for safe ways to get rid of nuclear waste.

THREE GORGES DAM

In China, a new dam is being built on the Yangtze river, the longest river in China. The dam will be used to make electricity. It will save 45 million tonnes of coal from being used. This will prevent air pollution.

▲ A model of the Three Gorges Dam, in China.

But the dam needs a reservoir that is 590 kilometres long and covers an area of 25,000 hectares. The reservoir must flood an area called the Three Gorges, a region of outstanding beauty. It will cover thirteen cities, 140 towns and hundreds of small villages. Over 2 million people will have to find new homes and millions of plants and animals will lose their habitat.

Many people do not think the dam should be built. Dai Qing, a journalist, spent ten months in prison because she wrote a book protesting against the dam.

Using fossil fuels

When engines in cars and other vehicles burn fossil fuels, they release gases into the atmosphere. These gases pollute the air and can form acid rain. They also affect the world's climate.

Global warming

Some scientists believe that burning fossil fuels is making the world's climate warmer. The earth has a layer of gases around it. These are called greenhouse gases, which act like a blanket and keep the earth warm. Burning fossil fuels is increasing these gases in the atmosphere and could be making the world hotter.

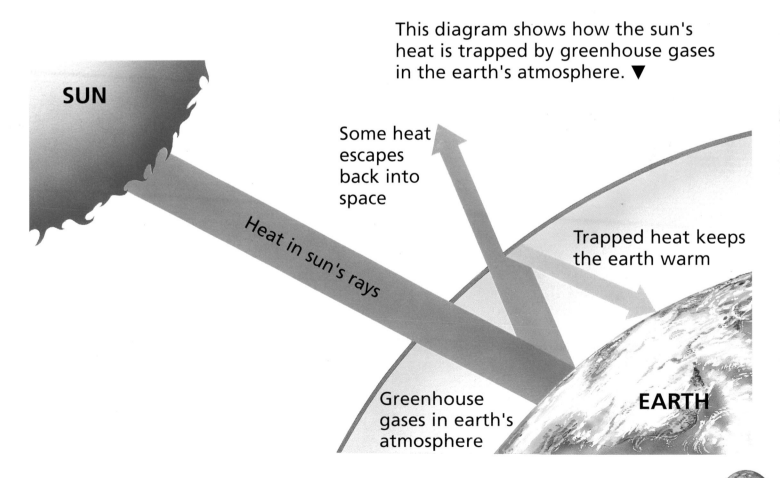

This diagram shows how the sun's heat is trapped by greenhouse gases in the earth's atmosphere. ▼

SUN

Some heat escapes back into space

Heat in sun's rays

Trapped heat keeps the earth warm

Greenhouse gases in earth's atmosphere

EARTH

The effects of global warming

Some people think the earth could get warmer by 3.5 degrees Celsius over the next 100 years. If this happens, huge areas of ice in the Arctic will melt and sea levels could rise by 50 cm. Areas near coasts would be flooded and small islands would be completely submerged.

A warmer climate would cause drought and water shortages. Crops could fail. This would cause famine, and millions of people could be forced to move to new regions.

A warmer climate could mean rivers like this one would run dry. ▼

Mosquitoes that carry malaria are only found in warm climates. They could spread to new areas. Wildlife that could not adapt fast enough would become extinct.

Acid rain

Acid rain is formed when gases from power stations and car engines are released into the atmosphere. The gases mix with water in clouds. When it rains, the rain is a weak acid mixture. It destroys trees and plants, and can kill wildlife in rivers.

◀ This tree has been killed by acid rain.

Activity

Lichen can be green, grey or brown. ▼

AIR POLLUTION SURVEY

Lichen is a type of plant that grows on trees, rocks and walls. It doesn't grow well in polluted air.

1. Look for lichen growing on a tree or a wall.

2. Find the place where it stops growing.

3. Look around to see what might be stopping it growing, for example pollution from traffic or factory chimneys.

How much energy?

You can find out how much energy you use in your home or school by looking at a meter. Electricity, gas and oil companies use meters to show how much we have used. Then they can calculate how much we have to pay. Energy is measured in joules.

Activity

SCHOOL ENERGY SURVEY

1. Make a list of everything in your school that uses energy and the type of energy it uses.

2. How does the energy come into the school buildings?

3. Where are the control switches?

4. Where are the meters and what do they show?

This woman uses energy in many different ways in her kitchen. How many machines can you see in the picture? ▶

Lots of energy

Wealthy, developed countries like Britain and the USA use much more energy than poorer countries. People in wealthier countries have more cars, computers and other machines. They have more money to buy the electricity and gas that runs the machines. But poorer countries are catching up.

▲ A street in Calcutta, in India. More and more people are buying cars in developing countries like India.

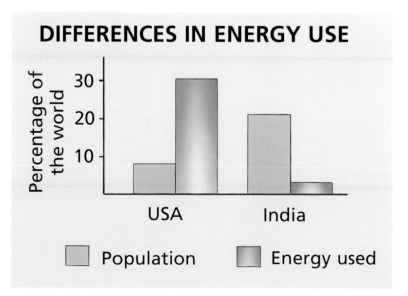

DIFFERENCES IN ENERGY USE

Percentage of the world

30

20

10

USA   India

◻ Population   ◻ Energy used

Not enough energy

In poorer, developing countries, many people still use wood for fuel. Trees are cut down for fuel. As trees disappear, villagers have to go further and further to collect firewood.

The roots of trees help to keep the soil in place when it rains. In areas where most of the trees have been cut down, the soil is eroded, or washed away. This makes it harder to grow crops.

People are trying to find other sources of energy to use as fuel, such as animal dung.

◄ A woman puts cow dung on to sticks to use as fuel.

CLOCKWORK RADIO

Most radios today use energy from electricity or from batteries. Both of these energy sources can pollute the environment. In poor countries some people cannot afford batteries.

An inventor called Trevor Baylis wanted to make a radio that everyone could afford, including people in the remote countryside in Africa. So he invented a radio that works by clockwork.

When the radio is wound up, energy is stored in a metal spring. As the spring slowly unwinds, it releases its energy and powers a generator. The Freeplay clockwork radio takes about 20 seconds to wind up and lasts for up to an hour.

▲ The Freeplay clockwork radio.

◄ Clockwork radios can be used in places where there is no electricity.

Using less energy

If we want to make sure there is enough energy in fifty years' time, we have to cut down the amount of energy we use. There are many ways to do this.

These women only have fuelwood for cooking. ▶

Wasting less energy

The simplest way of using less energy is not to waste any. Turn off lights when you leave a room. Switch off machines such as televisions and computers when they are not being used. Only use radiators in the rooms you are in. Fit insulation in roofs and around windows to stop heat escaping.

Governments

Governments can encourage people to use less energy by making them pay taxes on the energy they use. They can also encourage people to use public transport. This uses less energy per person than cars.

Governments can encourage energy companies to produce more energy from renewable sources such as wind, water and solar power.

TRUE STORY

A GREEN HEAT SCHEME IN BRITAIN

Rubbish is taken to be burned. ▼

The green heat scheme is run in Sheffield. It is a system of burning rubbish and producing power at the same time.

In the scheme, the city's rubbish is burnt and the heat is used to make steam. The steam is used to heat up homes, offices and other buildings. The steam is also used to make electricity.

Rubbish is used instead of fossil fuels to make energy. So the scheme prevents thousands of tonnes of gases from being released into the atmosphere.

This pipeline will carry hot water to the centre of Sheffield. ▶

Renewable energy

The world's population is growing. Developing countries are becoming industrialized. More and more energy is needed every day. This means that even if we find ways of cutting down the amount of energy we use at the moment, we still need to look for new, renewable sources of energy to use instead of fossil fuels.

These solar dishes collect energy from the sun. ▼

Renewable sources

Wind, wave and tidal power can make electricity by using the flow of air, water and tides to turn turbines.

Solar power traps the heat of the sun, and geothermal power uses the heat in rocks deep underground.

Other renewable energy sources include burning rubbish (see page 23), and burning wood from specially grown trees. This is called biomass.

▲ A tidal barrier and power station across the estuary of the Rance river, in France.

SOLAR-POWERED HOUSE

Bill and Debbi Lord live in Maine, in the USA. Their house makes its own solar power, using solar panels on the roof.

▲ The solar panels on this roof face the south, so they get sunshine all through the day.

The house has two types of solar panels. One type heats water and the other makes electricity. The water runs around the house in pipes, heating the radiators and providing hot water through the taps.

A ventilation system lets air out but keeps the heat in. The house also has an insulated roof and windows, so no heat is wasted.

At night, when there is no sunshine, Bill and Debbie use electricity supplied by their local electricity company. But in the daytime the house provides more electricity than they need, so the electricity company buys it from them.

The problems of renewable energy

Renewable energy sources do not release harmful gases into the atmosphere. But they can harm habitats when they are built and can change the look of a landscape.

When the barrage of a tidal power station is built across a river, it disturbs the river's wildlife. Wind turbines often cover a large area of land and some people think they spoil landscapes. Renewable energy can also be less reliable and more expensive than energy from fossil fuels.

Wind power is one of the cleanest forms of renewable energy. ▼

RENEWABLE ENERGY USE

In 2004, less than 4 per cent of the UK's electricity was made from renewable energy sources. By 2010, the Government's target is 10 per cent. To meet this target, approximately 5-10,000 wind turbines will be needed.

The future

We have found out that renewable sources of energy are less harmful to the environment than fossil fuels and that they will not run out. But it may take some time for renewable energy sources to completely replace fossil fuels.

Many developing countries are already building power stations that use renewable energy sources, such as hydropower. Wealthy countries, such as Britain and the USA, must also choose to use more renewable energy sources. This will protect the environment for people in the future.

Solar panels outside a hospital in Tanzania. ▼

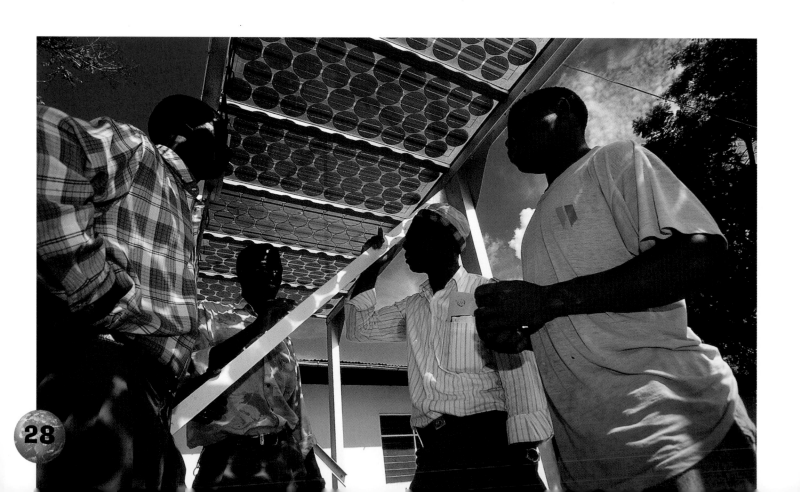

Activity

MAKE A SOLAR PANEL

1. Line the inside of a cardboard box with silver foil.
2. Cut a length of PVC tubing, three times the length of the box.
3. Fix the tubing into the box in a curvy shape, using wire to attach each bend.
4. Put a lump of Plasticine in one end of the tube and pour water in the other end.
5. Keeping the tube full of water, put the solar panel in a sunny place and leave it for a few hours.
6. Test the temperature of the water to see if it is warm.

How do you think the silver foil helped heat the tubing?

Which countries would solar power work best in?

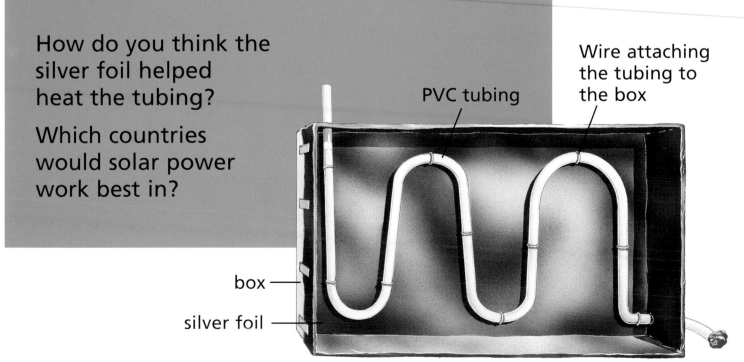

PVC tubing

Wire attaching the tubing to the box

box

silver foil

Glossary

Acid rain Rain that contains pollution from factories and traffic.

Atoms The tiny particles that make up every chemical.

Barrage An artifical barrier in a river.

Developed countries Wealthy countries where most people work in manufacturing or shops, banks, hotels and so on.

Developing countries Poorer countries where most people still work on farms and the industries are small.

Environment Everything in our surroundings, such as the earth, air and water.

Fossilized Made into a fossil. Fossil fuels are formed over millions of years from the remains of plants and animals.

Fuelwood Wood that is used as fuel, for cooking and heating.

Hydropower Energy made from moving water. It is also called hydroelectric power.

Industrialized Countries are industrialized when their business, manufacturing and trade industries have become very important.

Non-renewable Not replaceable. Coal, oil and gas are non-renewable sources of energy. They cannot be replaced as quickly as they are used up.

Renewable Able to be replaced. The wind, the sun and moving water are renewable sources of energy because they replace themselves as they are used. They will not run out.

Reservoirs Places where water is collected and stored.

Turbines Engines or motors that are made to work by the power of water, steam or air.

Further information

MUSIC
- Compose a song or rap to give a message about how people use energy

GEOGRAPHY
- Human use of energy around the world
- Extraction of resources
- Mapwork
- Environmental issues: global climate and sea level change, land use, land/water/air pollution

HISTORY
- Water power and mills
- invention of steam power
- Energy/pollution

ART & CRAFT
- Using energy as a stimulus for painting/modelling
- Design a poster on reducing energy use

Topic Web

DESIGN & TECHNOLOGY
- Simple machines and mechanisms to demonstrate energy transfer

MATHS
- Measuring of units of energy
- Simple statistics
- Graphs about energy use

SCIENCE
- Formation of fossil fuels
- Nuclear reactions and radioactivity
- Electriciy
- Environmental issues: e.g. habitat loss, damage to ecosystems

ENGLISH
- Using energy as a stimulus for creative writing
- Reports/letters
- Library skills

Other books to read

Action for the Environment: Energy Supplies by Chris Oxlade and Rufus Bellamy (Franklin Watts, 2004)

Alpha Science: Energy by Sally Morgan (Evans, 1997)

A Closer Look at the Greenhouse Effect by Alex Edmonds (Franklin Watts, 1999)

Essential Energy: Energy Alternatives by Robert Snedden (Heinemann, 2002)

Future Tech: Energy (Belitha, 1999)

Saving our World: New Energy Sources by N. Hawkes (Franklin Watts, 2003)

Science Topics: Energy by Chris Oxlade (Heinemann, 1998)

Step-by-Step Science: Energy and Movemont by Chris Oxlade (Franklin Watts, 2002)

Sustainable World: Energy by Rob Bowden (Hodder Wayland, 2003)

Index